Annie Creswick Dawson face-to-face with Benjamin Creswick's frieze for Cutlers' Hall, London (September 2015).

BENJAMIN CRESWICK

Annie Creswick Dawson

with Paul Dawson

Published by
The Guild of St George

Published 2015 by the Guild of St George Publications
10 St Oswald's Road, York YO10 4PF

www.guildofstgeorge.org.uk

ISBN 978-0-9932009-3-9

Design by Paul Dawson.

Technical assembly by Stuart Eagles.

Printed in Reading by Herald Graphics Ltd, 272 Elgar Road South.

This book is printed in accordance with Forest Stewardship Council standards. FSC certification provides a credible link between responsible production and consumption of forest products, enabling consumers and businesses to make purchasing decisions that benefit people and the environment as well as providing ongoing business value.

CONTENTS

List of Illustrations

Foreword

Paul Dawson

It is well known that John Ruskin supported, encouraged and advised many young men and women with their artistic ambitions. His patronage and connections secured many careers, and his years at the London Working Men's College brought significant opportunities to several young men out of the hundreds who attended. For some, the support was in developing naïve skills into something more refined and life-improving, and that alone was the purpose of his teaching. For a few others his support was financial, so that these young men could afford to spend the necessary time mastering their skills. That financial support was often significant and given to several recipients simultaneously, and it is hard to calculate the total cost to Ruskin of this generosity.

For some of those in receipt of such help a long and successful career followed, and their names have become familiar to us. In some instances, their children followed in the family business and there is a proud legacy. But with each succeeding generation, the link is weakened as direct and first-hand memories are reduced to vague family anecdotes. In some cases the family line has died out or has been diluted and the vital documentary evidence is now dispersed or lost. It is very special therefore when a link is not only maintained, but strengthened by the recording of the story, protecting the legacy and the preserving an archive of artefacts, letters and photographs.

Annie Creswick Dawson is the great granddaughter of Benjamin Creswick, the Sheffield knife grinder who became a sculptor under Ruskin's patronage and enjoyed a successful career at a time when the Arts & Crafts movement was in the ascendancy. His reputation brought a string of successive commissions and he eventually became an establishment figure, heading the department of sculpture at the Birmingham Art School and becoming a Professor at the Royal Birmingham Society of Arts.

But Benjamin Creswick differs from many of those other craftsmen in that he came to Ruskin's attention almost a generation later. Creswick was only just born when Ruskin began teaching at the Working Men's College and it was not until 1877 that Ruskin became aware of his talent. Creswick's success spanned the nineteenth and twentieth centuries, and throughout his career he continued to follow and expound his Ruskinian teaching, up to his death in 1946. He was possibly the last surviving craftsman with a direct link to John Ruskin.

Annie Creswick Dawson has been researching her great grandfather's story for many years, travelling thousands of miles to search libraries and archives to compile as much as can be found to shed light on Benjamin Creswick's life story. This is in addition to her quest to locate all the surviving carvings, terra cotta sculptures, bronzes, friezes, commercial and municipal wall decoration, metalwork and so much more.

Annie also maintains the website www.benjamincreswick.org.uk/

This introduction to the life and work of Benjamin Creswick offers an insight into the scope and breadth of his talent, uniquely told by Annie Creswick Dawson who continues to add to her own archive and thereby to our understanding.

Benjamin Creswick's sculpting tools. (Collection of Annie Creswick Dawson)

Acknowledgements

This work is a collaboration that brings together my own heritage with previous and ongoing research in order to expand and develop our knowledge of Benjamin Creswick's life. The experience of my own early years in the Ruskin-inspired workshop of Benjamin's son Charles has without doubt provided a valuable background to this exploration.

Of the many books, articles and newspaper reports quoted in the source notes, a number are contemporary with Benjamin Creswick and their authors' identities lost to us, but we are grateful to them for their reportage and opinions of his craft – as they understood it – in the context of their own time.

More recently, authors have looked farther afield as technology has opened new windows into other archives, in other countries. We are grateful to them for the light that they have shone into some otherwise dark corners by making their research available. I have had particular assistance from Mark Frost, who not only provided invaluable details from the Rosenbach Museum and Library archives regarding Ruskin's correspondence with Henry and Emily Swan, but also vital insight into the pivotal meeting of the minds of Ruskin and Creswick.

Another scholar, Simon Ogden, set out on Creswick's trail some years ago and brought together a considerable archive of notes and information in the preparation of a paper, to which Lianne Hackett added her own research and presented a collaborative paper at the International Symposium *John Ruskin, the Brantwood Years* in July 2000 at Bowland College, Lancaster University. Both Simon Ogden and Lianne Hackett have been generous in giving me access to their work and allowing me to quote extensively from it. Stuart Evans has also graciously shared his knowledge and research on the Century Guild.

For any publication of this kind to reach fruition depends on the assistance of the curators of the many organisations that I approached, and their permissions to quote from sources within their collections. Sincere thanks go to Louise Pullen at the Ruskin Galleries, Sheffield; to Professor Stephen Wildman and his curatorial staff at the Ruskin Library and Research Centre, Lancaster, with a special mention of Dianne Tyler, Assistant Curator, for her generous assistance.

I also thank the Birmingham Institute of Art and Design's archivist Fiona Waterhouse, for her unfailing help with its extensive Birmingham Municipal School of Art archive. The Royal Birmingham Society of Artists kindly made its records accessible to me and it has been a particular pleasure to work with the young volunteer and trainee archivists. I thank the Rosenbach Library in Philadelphia, U.S.A., the Leeds Library and Information Service, Sheffield and Birmingham Local History Libraries, and also the William Morris Gallery, Walthamstow, where Carien Kremer the Exhibitions and Collection Officer has given me invaluable help. Special thanks must go to the Worshipful Company of Cutlers, London, where John Allen the Assistant Clerk, and his successor Rupert Meacher, have been generous with their time and interest in this project. The Worshipful Company has generously given me permission to use images of the frieze. I also acknowledge the help of the Historic Chapels Trust, the Royal Academy, and the Victorian Society.

Lianne Hackett has been a knowledgeable and unfailingly supportive colleague from the beginning of my research, and her as yet unpublished research into Charles and Norah Creswick has been extensive. Christine Woolmer has given valuable help with genealogical research; Mr D Thompson's research has also informed my work, as has Kathleen Hughes and her Oxford Searchers Group which inspired my earlier random research to become more systematic. The Bromsgrove Society, and particularly Quintin Watt for work on the Bromsgrove Guild, and many others in a list far too long to name individually, have helped me and directed my path. To all of these people generous with their time and knowledge I am truly grateful.

Those same thanks go also to Ruth Nutter of the *Ruskin in Sheffield* project, and to my ever-growing circle of Sheffield colleagues and friends, Fay Musselwhite prominent among them. They have been a tower of strength and I am so proud to be re-forging the links between Walkley and the Creswicks. My gratitude must, as always, go to Peter Wong who enabled me to carry on this research.

Then there is the army of Companions, Ruskin scholars and archivists who have contributed over the years to my research, especially Dr James Dearden whose help with Ruskin portraits and many other subjects has been indispensable. Cedric Quayle and Peter Wardle's works on Bewdley have formed a unique contribution, and the support of John Iles in Bewdley has been unfailing.

To Stuart Eagles, secretary of the Guild, whose support and advice throughout has been invaluable, I give my warm thanks.

I thank Paul Dawson for his exceptional hard work, support, insight and professional advice without which this publication would have been far harder to produce.

Clive Wilmer, through his encouragement, brought about this publication, and the fact that as Master of the Guild he is promoting this and other studies of the hitherto peripheral figures to Ruskin Studies is a tribute to his insight and to the health and ongoing work of the Guild of St George and its care for the development and enrichment of Ruskin's legacy.

While I have been very fortunate in the generosity of many others, any errors or misinterpretations of information given are mine. Any images not credited are either from my own collection or with the permission of Peter Murray from his Creswick archive. Where it has not been possible to locate an owner it is presumed that they are in the public domain. Should this not be the case, apologies are offered for any unintentional infringement, and should such information be received steps will be taken to make an appropriate correction in any future publication.

Of the many footnotes, certain referenced sources appear frequently and the following form of abbreviation will be used.

Brantwood Diary: *The Brantwood Diary*, Helen Gill Viljoen, ed. (Yale University Press, 1971)

B.I.A.D: Birmingham Institute of Art & Design.

By Hammer and Hand: Crawford, Alan, ed. *By Hammer and Hand: The Arts and Crafts Movement in Birmingham*. (Birmingham Museum and Art Gallery, 1984.)

Creswick: (followed by page number) a lecture titled 'Sculpture in its Application to Architecture' by Benjamin Creswick recorded in *Transactions of the National Association for the Advancement of Art and its Application in Industry*, 1891.

Ogden: Simon Ogden Research Papers.

Rosenbach: The Rosenbach Museum and Library, Philadelphia.

Ruskin Foundation: (Ruskin Library, Lancaster University)

Works: (followed by volume and page number) *The Library Edition of the Works of John Ruskin*, Cook and Wedderburn ed. (London: George Allen, 1903-12).

Benjamin Creswick in his studio, undated.

Personal Recollections of My Great Grandfather

I spent the greater part of my formative years in my grandparents' studio in Edinburgh. The bronze nameplate on its door proclaimed it to be the workshop of an artist craftsman, a term my grandfather used deliberately in the age-old battle of craftsmen to see their work recognised as art. Charles Creswick (1883-1965) was both craftsman and artist; sculptor as well as bronze founder; designer and innovator as well as silversmith and metalworker. My grandmother, originally a piano teacher who had become a jeweller under my grandfather's tuition, worked in her own part of the studio although she was not mentioned in the description on the bronze doorplate.

Ruskin, whose ethos inspired everything that was done in that workshop, and who has been recognised as the prime catalyst for the Arts and Crafts movement, was present in our everyday lives, an inheritance passed down from my great grandfather Benjamin Creswick (1853-1946) – a man inspired directly by Ruskin who recognised in him 'a true and pure genius.'[1] In a further letter from Brantwood in 1879 Ruskin wrote:

> I am determined to bring you all to Coniston [Benjamin Creswick and his wife and children] and have you near me at all events for some weeks, in order to put you clearly on your road in work and thought.[2]

These early comments from Ruskin indicate his determination to make a real difference to Creswick's perceptions and allow him to realise his

---

1 Rosenbach: *Unpublished Letters from John Ruskin to Henry and Emily Swan 1877-1878, Volume V* [EL3. R956 Ms1, v. 6] 112. Brantwood 1877.

2 Ruskin Foundation: Ruskin to Creswick, May 27, 1879.

potential, as the following pages will demonstrate. I now see with every word I read of Ruskin, that he was the motivation of that workplace, directly informing Benjamin's careful instruction of his sons; he was present in their family life and in Benjamin's teaching, and he was vital to the life we led in Edinburgh.

The life I led in all my leisure hours was not that of an apprentice, as my parents were opposed to my becoming an artist or a craftswoman, but alongside the workforce I learned from about the age of seven to cut out the shapes of leaves and flowers from sheet silver with very sharp clippers – no blunt ended scissors and paper for me! I learned to use a file, to solder, to make the silver granules by heating the silver to melting point and catching the globules at just the right time, and all this while working at my own workbench with all manner of sharp and dangerous tools. It was a workplace where everyone learned to respect both the tools and the materials, and to learn practically their properties. There was never a serious accident that I can remember, despite the dangers of the unguarded, incandescently hot anthracite pot-bellied stoves that heated the workshops in winter, and the pots of sulphuric acid mixtures bubbling precariously on gas rings to darken the raw new silver before polishing. There was a room for meeting clients and taking meals, with the baby grand piano that belonged to my grandmother. She still occasionally played while my grandfather would sing – quite a Victorian salon at times – and my grandmother also had space for her workbench in this room. There was also a tiny kitchen, but the larger areas consisted of two workshops; one for small items, and another for larger pieces and the preparation of sculptures for casting. Then there were the foundry pits where I would watch the molten metal poured into the casts. It was a raw, rough, grubby and practical place, but from it came works of great beauty and variety, both useful and decorative. There was jewellery; copper and brass; silver church plate; vases and silver spoons and sculptures and items of all sorts. It was both the work of my grandfather and of the commissioned casting for other sculptors.

I feel Ruskin would have been pleased by both the variety and quality of design being achieved. He would have been delighted to see practical goods alongside the beautiful and purely decorative, and all being produced in his ideal of the 'good' workplace. Individual craftspeople worked on complete projects, living simply and contentedly, and in joy and harmony with the work they carried out. It was an absolutely perfect example of what he held dear to his heart and what, because of his recognition, support, teaching and mentoring of Benjamin Creswick, was our life. Although it has to be said that my years there were at the absolute nadir of Ruskin's popularity when almost everything Victorian was viewed with contempt, we were living a life completely inspired by him and his positive intervention in Benjamin's life.

Incised initials of Benjamin Creswick on his sculpting tools.
(Collection of Annie Creswick Dawson)

Prior to Ruskin's interest in his sculptural abilities, Benjamin Creswick had completed one large scale project in stone. Almost certainly through the influence of architect Henry Lomas (see page 13), Creswick received the commission for the façade of the extension of the Sheffield and Hallamshire Bank in Church Street, Sheffield.

It was reported in the Sheffield and Rotherham Independent of September 5, 1878 when the work had been completed that:

> The work is [. ..] from the designs [...] by Henry Lomas [...] The whole of the carving, including the Ionic capitals on front of the building and the coat of arms above the parapet, has been executed by Benjamin Creswick, a young grinder of this town, who is now under the fostering care of Mr Ruskin.

The time taken to produce in stone eight columns and the coat of arms prior to the building's completion places this work before Creswick's first contact with Ruskin, and represents his first work on a public building

The Early Years

...my only duty is to keep myself in active work and thought for the present needs of those around me[3]

Benjamin Creswick was born in 1853. The surviving records of his early years confirm his apprenticeship to the knife-grinding trade, but the reasoning behind that choice of career path is puzzling. Why would the son of an independent artisan, a successful spectacle frame maker, be apprenticed to a deadly trade in such a hazardous environment where the life expectancy would rarely have exceeded 30 years? In those limited working years it was very likely that he would have suffered from pervasive lung disease, and risked on a daily basis the possibility of being hideously maimed or even killed by the breaking or disintegration of his grinding wheel.

The 'Grinding Hull' where Creswick worked, was the place where 'edged tools' acquired their fine cutting edge on water-powered grinding wheels, with the grinder sat astride a wooden 'horsing' over the grinding stone holding the blade against the fast-moving wheel. Investigations into the cause of these stone wheels breaking up, apparently without prior warning, never reached any positive conclusion, so it was an ever-present hazard.

Although the lung disease associated with this work had been recognised as silicosis, or 'grinders disease,' caused by the inhalation of silicates in the stone dust, other lung problems occurred for which no cause was recognised. It is now understood that in the Grinding Hull, not only was a water container ever present at the grinder's side where he continually dipped the blade to keep it wet for the grinding process, but for some procedures the grinding wheel itself was partly immersed to provide a wet grinding surface. This water flew off the wheel in tiny droplets and was also breathed in by the grinders, and being continually recirculated it became the spawning ground for disease-carrying spores.[4]

There can be little doubt that the hard and uncomfortable working environment, coupled with the trauma of seeing friends and colleagues either desperately ill or injured, contributed to the reputation these men

---

[3] Moore, T. Sturge, and D.C. Sturge Moore, eds., *Works and Days, From the Journal of Michael Field.* (London: 1933) p.153. John Ruskin to Kathleen Bradley, in a letter dated February 1877.

[4] An account of the grinding process can be found at http://www.simt.co.uk/collections-and-displays

gained as being notoriously drunken, promiscuous and profligate with high rates of absenteeism.[5]

In the Grinding Hull; a section of the images on the Cutlers Hall Frieze, London 1888. The seated figure fifth from the left is almost certainly a self-portrait of Benjamin Creswick grinding the blade of a table knife.

Creswick's family was reasonably well off, and not living in the impoverished back-to-back housing in the smoke-filled lower parts of Sheffield where the foundries and Grinding Hulls were situated, so it is something of a mystery that he should have been 'sent like fuel to feed the factory smoke.'[6] This, like many other aspects of his early life, may remain an unanswered question. However, we do know that he continued as a knife grinder until after his marriage to Fanny Goodhall in 1873,[7] and that he had begun to show the early signs of lung disease. Visiting a local doctor, Dr Balbirnie[8], he was strongly advised to either leave knife grinding or face an inevitable and painful death from lung disease. A visit to a doctor was unusual owing to cost, which suggests the help of a patron, because more commonly a herbalist, or 'wise woman' might have been the expected source of assistance. The doctor, evidently a benevolent man, asked if he had any other skills by which he might earn a living, and Creswick produced from his pocket a small portrait bust of Dante modelled in terra cotta. This must have been something of a surprise to the good doctor, who was so impressed by the work that he commissioned a bust of himself from Creswick.

This story brings into question the oft-repeated tale that Ruskin had plucked Creswick quite untutored from the Grinding Hull; however

[5] Ogden.

[6] *Works*: 10, p. 193. (Chapter 6, 'The Nature of Gothic').

[7] T. Raffles Davison: *Sheffield and Rotherham Independent.* May 4, 1887.

[8] Ibid.

heart-warming and beneficent that may sound, we must question its accuracy.

As part of his effort to find a way out of knife grinding, Creswick had already been attending sculpture classes run by the First West York Engineers which were founded by the Sheffield School of Art. This would have been where Creswick met the architect Henry Dent Lomas (right) modelled by Creswick in 1876, who was teaching at the Art School and is likely to have been the benefactor known to have given Creswick access to his personal library of art books.[9] He was a well-known supporter of young artists in Sheffield and it may well have been him who paid for Creswick's visit to Dr Balbirnie. Creswick had been tutored there by a Mr Read Turner who, besides being a

volunteer, worked at the Sheffield School of Art. Creswick exhibited at the Sheffield Society of Artists in 1876 and received a positive review in the local newspaper: 'B.C., a grinder who manifests a good deal of rough talent in several medallion portraits which by no means disgrace the exhibition.'[10] It was the same enthusiastic, although perhaps inexperienced sculptor who had turned up at the Walkley Museum when it opened in 1875, the portal through which John Ruskin intended to feed the minds of the working men of Sheffield. One of the museum's greatest achievements was the transformation of Benjamin Creswick's life.

In 1877 he had been visiting the Museum long enough to have caught the attention of Henry and Emily Swan, the curators of what Creswick must have seen as a wonderful house of inspirational treasures, and it is very possible that it was the Swans' encouragement that persuaded him to exhibit in 1876. There is, however, no doubt that it was the Swans

[9] *Biographical notes and list of the principal works of Henry Dent Lomas 1819-1901.* Leaflet in the collection of the Sheffield Local History Library.

[10] *Sheffield and Rotherham Independent*, Thursday May 25, 1876, p6. Sheffield Society of Artists Exhibition.

who made sure that Ruskin got to hear about Creswick's work, because in June 1877 Ruskin had wrote from Brieg replying to a letter from Emily Swan: 'That sculptor is, I doubt not, a real one and will come to much good'[11].

Keen to follow up on Ruskin's encouraging response, the Swans lent Creswick a photograph of Ruskin from which he was able to model a small portrait bust. Possibly this was the object of a visit on 22 August 1877 by the Swans, which Ruskin records in his Brantwood diaries as troubling: 'A quite frightful fit of depression brought on by my curator and his wife coming when they shouldn't.'[12]

Whatever distress Ruskin felt soon dissipated and Creswick was invited to Brantwood in September to begin a portrait bust of Ruskin from life. This was to be the first life sculpture of Ruskin, which in itself was a rare privilege, but to grant the necessary time to this young man does suggest Ruskin's belief in the sculptor's potential. However, Ruskin's diary entry on the day reveals his downcast mood: '...had the sculptor from Sheffield, but sadly tired for want of any *sort* of rest all day, for I was thinking of him as a problem all the while he worked.'[13] However, it was not Creswick, but other events in Ruskin's life that caused his melancholy state. When Creswick was asked how many sittings he required, he asked for five. Ruskin's reply was that from what he had seen of the work, Creswick could have as many as he liked[14] – a great encouragement to the young sculptor. It is worth drawing attention to a letter written from Venice in February 1877 to Katherine Bradley, a Companion of the Guild of St George, in which Ruskin wrote:

> My real pleasure, so far as any is left me now in this [world], is [...] in being useful, above all in teaching or comforting people who can be easily taught or greatly comforted [...] my only duty is to keep myself in active work and thought for the present needs of those around me[15]

[11] Rosenbach: [EL3. R956 MS1, v4] 94 JR, Brieg 11.06.77.

[12] Brantwood Diary*:* p. 42.

[13] Brantwood Diary: p. 48.

[14] MH Spielmann, *John Ruskin* (London: Cassell & Co.1900) p. 176.

[15] Moore, T. Sturge, and D.C. Sturge Moore, eds., *Works and Days, From the Journal of Michael Field.* (London: 1933) p.152, 153.

Ruskin portrait bust by Benjamin Creswick, 1877.
(Collection of the Guild of St George)

Benjamin Creswick may have been, to Ruskin's eyes, an ideal candidate for such 'teaching and comfort.' Having recognised in Creswick what he repeatedly referred to as a 'pure and true genius', Ruskin began to consider the role of patron and mentor. Unfortunately, 1878 brought Ruskin other pressures and health concerns that temporarily frustrated this good intention, but nevertheless he 'saw help given to Sheffield's Mr Creswick.'[16] At the end of August we see Ruskin writing to George Baker at Bewdley and being 'most grateful [...] to you for employing Creswick who has the truest of genius, though it will take time to develop in the direction of beauty, but St George and you could not do greater kindness than in fostering it.'[17]

[16] Brantwood Diary p.49. Entry for September 15, 1877.

[17] *Works*: 30, p. 302.

Ruskin's protégé also found some work for himself at Bewdley, however, and 'might almost be counted as a Bewdley Companion in view of his local work in general and the Beaucastle sculptures in particular'[18] We know that his work included a carved sign or panel for the 'Black Boy Inn,' but records of other projects have not yet been located. He took accommodation for himself and his family in Bewdley at 7, High Street[19] and the Creswick's third child Benjamin was born in Bewdley in 1878. However it is the sculptures For George Baker's new house, 'Beaucastle,' that were to be the most significant.

Creswick went to Beaucastle after the main building work was finished and we have Edith Hope Scott's published account of the Guild to thank for the description of the immediate outcome of this commission. Baker gave Creswick the opportunity to express his Ruskin-inspired skills in carving and this can be seen as work done in the true gothic tradition, *in situ*, that Hope Scott so eloquently described as:

> The beautiful stone carving in the Wyre Forest red sandstone [...] `He carved the capitals of the short pillars in the outside stone staircase with the wildlife of the forest – squirrel and rabbit, deer and bird, among the oak and wild growth of the wood. Work delightful to himself and everyone who sees it.[20]

Creswick's recent studies with Ruskin spoke plainly through his work in observing truth to nature with its clear expression in his work. Along with the joy he took in it and shared with his viewers it is a tribute to both master and student, and a glimpse of the communication between them.

Ruskin's introduction of Creswick to George Baker would have an important and long lasting effect on Creswick's career. This was immediate through the Bewdley commission, but in having George Baker's support Creswick would later benefit from Baker's continuing involvement in the Guild of St George, his Birmingham civic connections, and those with the Birmingham Municipal School of Art, which would figure so strongly in his later career.

With the Whistler trial scheduled for November 25 1878, Ruskin's mind was fully occupied, but he found time to write to Creswick on November 14:

---

[18] Peter Wardle and Cedric Quayle, *Ruskin and Bewdley* (Guild of St George, 1989 and 2007) p.35.

[19] Ibid.

[20] Edith Hope Scott, *Ruskin's Guild of St. George* (Methuen 1931) p. 91.

> It is because I have more to say to you than to any other of my friends at present, that I can't begin saying anything: and put off from my day to day even telling you how truly I rejoice in your success and how grieved I am that I failed in contributing to it – I trust I am now able to redeem my words a little to you – only believe me, yet – though only in words and also, few enough of them! [21]

In this letter, Ruskin suggests that his recognition may have been a little late in arriving, but that amends would follow.

Creswick's attendance is recorded at the inaugural meeting of the Guild of St George on February 21, 1879.[22] Ruskin's interest in Creswick was also reignited that year, judging that it would be better to have Creswick close by if he was to teach him effectually. On 27th May 1879 Ruskin wrote:

> I am determined to fetch you all to Coniston and to have you near me at all events for some weeks, in order to put you clearly on your road in work and thought. Please come on Saturday and if I have not got the lodgings ready I will get ones elsewhere but I think that the lodgings will be ready: you have <u>two</u> children I think. I hope that the air will be as good for them & for your wife as any Shropshire breezes and the flowers are waiting to be modelled. – Have you the money to come?[23]

That same month Creswick moved to Coniston with his family and settled in lodgings with a Mrs Milligan.[24]

Ruskin is said to have supported Creswick and his family for some four years. We have an idea of that generosity from M.H. Spielmann: '[Ruskin] charging himself with the cost of their worldly necessities' and '[paying] all expenses, not only for himself during four years, but also for his family [...] and his aged parents.'[25] But having agreed to finance a studio in Coniston for Creswick and paying a living allowance, their relationship was temporarily marred when Mrs Milligan's bill for lodging was presented to Ruskin, which drew this undated reply:

> I was sadly tired yesterday and very cross, first at being so absurd as to go tumbling about after plants, which grow as thick as hay under your feet everywhere – and secondly at getting a bill for the lodgings [at] Mrs Milligan's which I fully understood were to be paid by you – I don't at all mean to pay you £7 a month & lodgings too!

---

[21] Ruskin Foundation: Ruskin to Creswick from Brantwood, November 14, 1878.

[22] Mark Frost. *The Lost Companions and the Guild of St George*. Anthem Press, 2014, p.194. The Roll of the Guild records that he was admitted as a Companion in December 1884.

[23] Ruskin Foundation: Ruskin to Creswick from Brantwood, May 27, 1879.

[24] This is Frances Milligan, born c. 1846. Her husband, Joseph, was an ostler. They probably lived then, as in 1881, at Dixon Ground, Coniston.

[25] M.H. Spielmann, *John Ruskin* (London: Cassell & Co.1900) p. 176.

> The studio I said I would pay for but not the lodgings – however I've written to Dr Parsons to come and look after you and will clear Mrs Milligan but it can't go on so.[26]

Ruskin's diary entries show visits to Creswick's studio during that year, but with no details on the nature of the visits.[27] There must have been many more visits than he recorded in his diary if he was to have encouraged and instructed his protégé. During this period Creswick made a number of visits to Sheffield, no doubt to visit his extended family, besides visits to the Museum at Walkley where his name regularly appears in the visitors' book. And, of course, to visit his mentors, Henry and Emily Swan.

Besides teaching Creswick himself, Ruskin also sought patrons and commissions for him. Included in this was Ruskin's plan to '...set Creswick to work on carving the marble facings'[28] for his projected museum in Sheffield.

These early days, when Ruskin was guiding Creswick's new life as a sculptor, established the ethics, honed the skills and developed the vision that constantly motivated and inspired Creswick – not merely throughout his career as a sculptor and teacher – but throughout his whole life.

They enabled him to achieve his stated aim of making buildings 'sparkle with interest.' They also became the cherished inheritance of his sons, trained by him in Birmingham at the School of Art, and who worked alongside him in the family studio in the garden of their Sutton Coldfield home.

Benjamin Creswick's sculpting tools.
(Collection of Annie Creswick Dawson)

[26] Ruskin Foundation: Ruskin to Creswick from Brantwood, 1879.

[27] Brantwood Diary: pp. 180, 192, 202.

[28] Rosenbach: *Unpublished Letters from John Ruskin to Henry and Emily Swan 1879-1887, Volume VII* [EL3. R956 MS1, v.7] 144 Brantwood, 15 02.79.

Mr Creswick of London

Creswick's move to London remains obscure in its details. What is clear is that Ruskin had plans to employ Creswick as a sculptor on his proposed museum whether it should be in Sheffield or at Bewdley. Sheffield was the more likely choice, although undated letters make the position unclear. As early as November 1877, Ruskin was writing to Emily Swan from Oxford about the purchase of marble for Creswick to work on under his direction. A letter to Henry Swan on 15th February 1879, records his intention.

> … I will desire the chairman at the meeting on the 21st to ask you to state to the meeting the necessity for a museum building. They must get me some [land] and I'll soon design it, and set Creswick to carve. I mean to do it. St, Mark's way – brick with marble casing, so I can get my inner walls dry at once, and go on at leisure adding panel by panel of decoration.[29]

But as work in Bewdley did not immediately materialise, Creswick decided that a move to London might well advance his career, ensuring that he could keep his growing family fed and housed. There is no firm record to tell us whether Ruskin's initial generosity of four years' support was still in place, or had by then expired. London would certainly be seen as a possible option, while a return to work on the Museum, either at Sheffield or later at Bewdley, could be managed, but Ruskin's intentions on this are not clear.

Creswick was readily welcomed in London by the architect and designer, Arthur Heygate Mackmurdo (1851-1942) and was widely accepted among Ruskin's followers. This suggests either an introduction from Ruskin, or at the very least, advance notice of his arrival, and with it a recommendation of Creswick's skill and potential. Mackmurdo had met Ruskin some years earlier and had joined him on tour in Italy in 1874, having previously studied at Lambeth Drawing School. Ruskin set him to work drawing both natural scenes and architecture under his instruction, and a year later Mackmurdo had set up his practise as an architect. At the time of Creswick's arrival in London, he was living and working at 20, Fitzroy Street in Camden.

Creswick is recorded as living in the Mackmurdo house in 1880, and later at Hollyplace, Enfield. He had quickly been integrated into the

---

[29] Rosenbach: *Unpublished Letters from John Ruskin to Henry and Emily Swan1879-1887, Volume VII* [EL3. R956 Ms1, v. 7] 144. I am indebted to Mark Frost for directing me to this evidence.

group of artists and craftsmen who were to form the Century Guild: Herbert Horne (1864-1916), Selwyn Image (1849-1930), Clement Heaton (1861-1940) and William de Morgan (1839-1917). The number of Creswick's recorded works from that time demonstrates his prolificacy, so it must have been an intensely inspiring company he was keeping. He was described as 'a happy, gregarious and collaborative craftsman'[30] and was in his element working in his favourite medium, terra cotta.

The earliest work from this period in London seems to be the Mackmurdo bronze mantelpiece dated 1880; a major collaborative piece, with Benjamin Creswick's decorative panels set into a fireplace of Mackmurdo's design (typical of his architectural style of furniture). It must have been of a considerable weight.

The panels are a resounding declaration of Creswick's intent as a sculptor to portray the dignity of everyday work and its place at the heart of daily family life, the values that would influence him throughout his career.

In 1882, Creswick was collaborating closely with Mackmurdo; his terra cotta portrait bust of Mackmurdo dated 1882 is in the William Morris Gallery.[31] Their records suggest that it was probably sculpted in Mackmurdo's house at 20 Fitzroy Street. It was given to the collection in 1942, and exhibited in the Birmingham City Art Gallery's exhibition, *Masterly Art: The Birmingham School of Art,* in 1986-7.

By 1883, the Creswick family appears to have settled for a short time at Hollyplace, in Enfield, where another son, Charles, was born in 1883.

The following year a report about the Enfield Local Art exhibition of May/June 1884 revealed that: 'Mr Benjamin Creswick of Hollyplace, Enfield, was a large exhibitor of sculpture. A portrait bust of the noted John Ruskin taken from life was greatly admired, as was the Child's Head, a portrait bust of the son of Mr D'Oyly Carte, of the Savoy theatre, taken from life.'[32]

The report continued that: 'The Blacksmith'[33] in terra cotta attracted a good deal of attention and, as one of the speakers observed at the opening of the exhibition, it was 'worthy of a young Flaxman...' John Flaxman, R.A. (1775-1826) was a successful sculptor of terra cotta

---

[30] The Sheffield and Rotherham Independent, April 20, 1889.

[31] William Morris Gallery catalogue number SC 32, Bust of Arthur Heygate Mackmurdo, incised on right shoulder Benjamin Creswick/sc./1882.

[32] Meyers Observer. June 14, 1884 report of the exhibition.

[33] Now in the collection of the William Morris Gallery having been donated in 1950 by Frank Brangwyn.

reliefs, medallions and memorials, later associated with Josiah Wedgwood and the modelling of reliefs for use on the company's jasperware and basalt ware. Such a comparison was true praise indeed. The same reviewer went on, '...The medallion heads for the Leeds Reading Room: Homer, Dante particularly good, Macaulay and Goethe, were by the same gentleman as were a number of busts and panels.'

Medallion head of Dante for the Leeds Reading Room, 1884.

It is interesting to note that in the records about the Leeds commission, Creswick had become 'Mr Creswick of London' and had ceased to be the 'Sheffield grinder.' That soubriquet had followed him throughout his later career in the Midlands, continuing to provide an engaging 'rags to riches' story that appealed to the press, linking his untutored skill to recognition by Ruskin, and his subsequent success.

In that same year, Creswick also exhibited at the Autumn Exhibition of Modern Pictures (Walker Art Gallery, Liverpool). In 1885, he exhibited a model of the portrait roundel of Carlyle which was to be placed within a decorative panel by Charles Voysey (1857-1941) on Carlyle's house in Cheyne Row. In 1886, he exhibited once more at Liverpool. By now he was recorded as being established in a studio in Newman Street, Camden Town, a few streets away from Mackmurdo's loose commune of artists in his Fitzroy Street home.[34] Creswick shared his studio for a short time with Frank Brangwyn (1857-1956) who himself was a protégé of Mackmurdo.

---

[34] Ogden.

Portrait of Carlyle placed within a decorative panel by Charles Voysey (1857-1941) on Carlyle's house in Cheyne Row.
Picture courtesy of the *Victorian Web.*

He became a lifelong friend. Brangwyn would later write a tribute to Creswick in the *Birmingham Post* on his death in 1946. (From my childhood, I remember two wonderful bronze bookends by Brangwyn. I wonder if Benjamin or my grandfather cast them and where they are now?)

Creswick is thought to have been formally recognised as an associate of the Century Guild at this time, and although at present it cannot be confirmed, Creswick's appointment as modeller for the Guild around the time of the Liverpool exhibition seems to suggest this was the case.

There are records of his having exhibited at the first exhibition of the Arts and Crafts Exhibition Society in 1888 with other members of the Century Guild. This was, of course, the now famous New Gallery Exhibition of the autumn of 1888 when the term 'arts & crafts' was first applied to the movement. The recently formed Art Workers' Guild had been drawing support from many names now familiar to us. Specifically, it was co-founded by Walter Crane (1845-1915) who sought to find a public platform for the artists' ideals. No tangible progress had been made towards achieving this aim when, in 1886, a number of activists that included Heywood Sumner (1853-1940), Henry Holiday (1839-1927), T.M. Rooke (1842-1942), W.A.S. Benson (1854-

1924) and Walter Crane proposed the idea for an exhibition that would have the title, 'The Combined Arts.' That seemingly pedestrian title was amended to the more resonant 'Arts and Crafts Exhibition Society' and history was made. The press picked up on the name, and the event cannot be described as anything but a success. The better-known artists such as William de Morgan, W.A.S. Benson, Heywood Sumner, Burne-Jones and of course Walter Crane were trumpeted, but the Century Guild was also recognised and the wide range of its respective talents noted, among them, Benjamin Creswick.

Simon Ogden records that, typical of Creswick's prolific output, he exhibited twelve of the Guild's total of thirty-two exhibits. An examination of the titles of his works reveals immediately his commitment to the theme of work and family life in England. Creswick's 'Man with a Scythe' is a beautiful piece demonstrating a profound understanding of man and his work; how a man holds his tools and how he stands as he uses them. This is both the result of a sculptor's intensive observational study and a man's personal experience of using heavy implements, and knowing for himself their weight and swing. This was Creswick's great advantage. His work conveys his understanding of the man's stance, balance, power and the ease that comes only with experience.

Creswick began taking commissions in London following his successes at the exhibition. One was the frieze for the shop front of Heath the Hatters, then at 105-109 Oxford Street. In the *British Architect,* in a series of *Studies of Street Architecture,* T. Raffles Davison (himself an architect and the illustrator of the article) described Creswick's frieze as 'about the best architectural feature in a shop front which can be seen in any London Street and [...] marks a development of Creswick's style – the figures are in lower relief and are more integrated into the building's overall design.'[35]

It is interesting to record that when first offered the commission, Creswick refused as he knew nothing about the hat-making process. The proprietor persuaded him to spend a few weeks in the factory (situated behind the Oxford Street store) watching and learning, and Creswick agreed – Ruskin's teaching on the truth of work and careful observation bringing success to the venture.

---

[35] *British Architect*. 'Studies of Street Architecture,' illustration No. 13 by T. Raffles Davison, 1888.

Frieze above the shop front of Heath the Hatters, Oxford Street.

Another London commission resulted in one of Creswick's major works. The terra cotta frieze for the Cutlers' Hall (The Worshipful Company of Cutlers) at Warwick Lane covers a length of 31 feet and a depth of 2 ft. 9 inches and is filled with powerful images that reflect the reality of the Cutler's trade. It graphically depicts the different stages of the various processes in all their vigour and danger, mixing power and vulnerability. It is examined more fully in the chapter *Key Works*, on p. 37. All that is added here are the words of E.T. Cook in the Library Edition of Ruskin's Works:

> The interest and vitality of this latter work are as remarkable as is the beauty of its grouping. As Ruskin would have wished, it takes its motive, not from past conventions, but from the actual life of the forge and the grindstone, as the artist himself knew it. The frieze – which illustrates successively the processes of smithing, grinding, finishing and fitting – is an attempt to show the interest and beauty which may surround the life and work of the skilled English mechanic.[36]

It is tempting to suggest that with this frieze alone, Creswick's place in the history of British art was assured.

[36] *Works*: 30, p.xlvi.

Birmingham

Buildings should sparkle with interest [37]

That Creswick was well established in London's Arts and Crafts world, gaining large commissions and working with leading design firms, is demonstrated by his burgeoning career. As well as his work with the Century Guild artists and craftsmen, he travelled to Manchester, Liverpool, and Leeds, working and exhibiting in all of these centres. Another significant event was that Creswick exhibited for the first time at the 1888 Royal Academy Summer Exhibition with a figure entitled 'Manly pride: study of a smith at work.' It is typical of the confidence he felt in his work, with its arguably unfashionable focus on the 'Dignity of Labour,' that he believed it would be accepted by the Royal Academy.

The blossoming of his career was evidently noted in Birmingham, where the Birmingham Municipal School of Art was about to choose a master for its new modelling department. An excellent book produced by Birmingham City Museum and Art Gallery, edited by Alan Crawford, describes the 'Birmingham Setting' in some detail.[38] There were many of Ruskin's admirers in the Birmingham circles of art and education, and prominent among them was George Baker (1825-1910) who had been a Mayor of Birmingham from 1876 and would later become the Mayor of Bewdley, thus taking a pivotal role in both locations of Ruskinian activity. Baker was a member of the appointments committee of the School of Art and had worked with many of the leading Arts and Crafts figures in the city. He was also acquainted with several wealthy philanthropic individuals who were interested in Ruskin and the Guild of St George, among them members of the Quaker Cadbury family and Unitarian Nettlefolds.[39] There was also Samuel Timmins (1826-1902), the nonconformist button manufacturer and antiquarian, and the architect, John Henry Chamberlain (1831-1883), both of whom were Companions. The most prominent Ruskinian of all, John Howard Whitehouse (1873-1955), was a founding member and life-long Secretary of the Ruskin Society of Birmingham in 1896.

---

[37] Creswick, p. 217.

[38] *By Hammer and Hand*: pp. 27-39.

[39] Frost 2014, p. 131.

It would seem unsurprising, then, that Creswick, whose work and career had first been encouraged by Ruskin and then promoted by George Baker, was considered for the post. There is no doubt that Creswick, as a Companion of the Guild, was known to many of these influential people, and he would later be commissioned by the Cadbury family to work in Bournville, the 'model village' created by the Cadbury brothers, for their workers in the green fields outside the city. The fact that Creswick's work had formed such a prominent part of the first Arts and Crafts exhibition, coupled with the fact that he had served as modeller to the Century Guild, led to him being sought for the position in 1888. Creswick was approached, and after a twenty per cent increase to the initial salary proposed, and an agreement that the School would allow him to fulfil standing commitments, he took up the position in the following January and brought his family back to the Midlands where he was to start a new career in teaching.[40]

The Birmingham Municipal School of Art (now known as the Birmingham Institute of Art and Design) retains Creswick's teaching record in their archive.[41]

He was seen as one of the key figures from outside Birmingham who could further the growing Arts and Crafts ideals within the School of Art[42]. Creswick was also to continue to develop his career in sculpture for over thirty years.

Following a few more changes of address that included a short stay in Manchester, where the seventh of the Creswick children was born, the family moved to Birmingham in 1888. That Manchester diversion may well have been the result of the Century Guild's collaboration on 'a set of rooms' in the Jubilee exhibition of 1887. There is a 'Buffet' (a sideboard or recessed cupboard stylised by Mackmurdo) dated 1896,[43] with a decoration by Benjamin Creswick in the Manchester Museums and Galleries, perhaps a survival from related Century Guild commissions from the following years.

---

[40] BIAD: Fiona Waterhouse. *Notes on Sources related to Benjamin Creswick, Minute books.* The notes referring to the appointment of Creswick are from a meeting in December 1888. He was appointed in 1888 and started work on 14th January 1889.

[41] B.M.S.A. (Birmingham Municipal School of Art) Management sub-committee Minutes 10, 1906-1908, Birmingham City University Art and Design Archive, SA/AD/2/10, page xx.

[42] *By Hammer and Hand*: p. 38.

[43] Manchester City Art Gallery Collection 1885, 1886. 39: Buffet by Arthur Heygate Mackmurdo. The Gallery is currently digitising its records, so full details are not at present available.

The Creswick family moved around in Birmingham until 1903 when they settled in Jockey Road, Sutton Coldfield, where a studio was set up.[44] In 1913 they moved to Elmwood, another house in Jockey Road, where Benjamin and his wife settled for the rest of their lives.

Creswick arrived in Birmingham with his usual enthusiasm and adaptability, and he took great delight in teaching, which was reflected in the success of his pupils. Ogden and Hackett state that within a year of his commencement, the School was winning the major share of the national modelling awards, and his teaching was praised by Walter Crane in his role as visiting inspector.[45] According to Frank Brangwyn's tribute Creswick was instrumental in the building of the new art laboratories in Colwell Street contributing panels for the tympani,[46] which perhaps may not be considered his most inspired work. But the success of his classes was not entirely without controversy. Under Creswick, the Art School achieved its aim of switching its focus to a more practical form of study rather than the merely academic, but the changes drew criticism from one of the examiners who claimed that the work was not fit for submission.

In an impassioned letter written in defence of his class of 1897, Creswick explained that the prize winners of the previous year were drawn only from the advanced classes, which consisted of only three students. For the current year, there were twenty students, and of that number, ten were first-year students, and many of the remaining ten were less experienced in figure modelling – the most difficult of the disciplines. Comparisons between previous and current results were, Creswick claimed, unfair to both his students and to himself. He went on to argue that his job, as he saw it, was not to concentrate on producing prize winners, but 'teaching my students to perceive what they are looking at, to understand [what] the qualities possessed consist of, to arouse the admiration for those qualities which alone will enable them to understand them;'[47] surely an echo of Ruskin's 'teaching one and the same thing to all, namely *Sight*. Not a slight thing to teach, this: perhaps on the whole, the most important thing to be taught in the whole range of teaching.'[48]

---

[44] Ogden, 1983.

[45] Hackett 2000, referencing Ogden 1983. A paper originally presented as part of the International Symposium *John Ruskin, the Brantwood Years* 18-20 July 2000, Lancaster University.

[46] *Birmingham Post*, February 13, 1946.

[47] B.I.A.D.: Fiona Waterhouse ref: Letter, Creswick to Preston Hytch, 1897.

[48] *Works*: 15, p. 177-201. Inaugural address at the Cambridge School of Art 1858.

Creswick had evidently taken to heart those very points that Ruskin had raised in his inaugural speech at the Cambridge School of Art. One can reasonably suppose that Ruskin's own recognition of inspired work in art and his enjoinder to 'never demand exact finish for its own sake but only for some practical or noble end' gave Creswick an understanding of the importance of this approach.[49] That ideal may, however, have been less persuasive to the examiner. Creswick stood by his and Ruskin's arts and crafts principle of 'truth to material' and competently withstood the setback, forging ahead with continuing success.[50] Creswick's Birmingham teaching can be seen as a continuation of Ruskin's teaching, but with Creswick's personal approach added to it, which was in turn passed on to the Birmingham Municipal School of Art students and to Creswick's sons who, in different degrees, followed in their father's footsteps. Most notable were Charles Creswick (1883-1965), and for perhaps a shorter time, his brother, John (b.1881 and recorded as active 1901-22.[51] Date of death not currently established) who both went to Edinburgh in 1913 to fulfil a commission from the Marquis of Bute.

Creswick's output seems to have diminished somewhat in the early years of his teaching, which is hardly surprising as he was settling into his new career. The wonderful example of Ruskin's teaching, combined with passion for his subjects, provided Creswick with a ready means of connecting with his students. Commissions continued to come, however, and the 'Elves and Shoemakers' is one of his earliest in Birmingham.[52] Sadly lost during redevelopment of Albert Street in 1985, it was a charming example of his determination to use his public sculpture to inform and teach, as well as to delight both children and adults. Placed over the corner doorway of Morton's shoe and boot manufacturing premises, it depicted the fairy tale from the Brothers Grimm with two elves hammering at the shoes, framed by sinuous roots and foliage.

As Creswick's personal work continued alongside his teaching, the success of his career might in part be assessed in terms of his challenge to the Birmingham craftsmen, as a number of complaints to the School

---

[49] Wilmer, Clive, ed. *Unto this Last and Other Writings*. Penguin Classics, 1997 pp.88 and 89.

[50] BIAD. Fiona Waterhouse (Research Assistant [archives]) ' Sources related to Benjamin Creswick'.

[51] John Creswick *Mapping the Practice*. University of Glasgow.

[52] George Noszlopy, *Public Sculpture of Birmingham Including Sutton Coldfield*. (Liverpool University Press, 1998) p.159.

of Art attest. In 1906, the Secretary of the local branch of the Wood Carvers, Modellers and Stone Carvers Union wrote to complain about Creswick undertaking modelling and other work on a number of buildings in the city in direct competition with their own members. They argued that 'in view of the salary he received from the School he should be debarred from such work and give all his time to his duties as a teacher.'[53] In response, the School committee informed the Union that they had never adopted such an approach and that, on the contrary, they regarded it as highly desirable that the teachers in their employment should actually practice the arts and crafts they teach. Further complaints later in the year resulted in no change to that policy.[54]

Examination of Creswick's sculpture, stone carving and metalwork reveals not only a substantial body of work, but the considerable diversity of its range. The scope and nature of his talents is touched upon in an article written in 1906 in the *Birmingham Magazine:*

> He is equally at home with a colossal sculpture, a memorial monument, or an architectural frieze as with an ivory statuette; a pair of gates or an inkstand in wrought iron, a silver and enamel loving cup and a watch case. The material matters not – a memorial in bronze, a granite carving, a carving in oak, monuments in marble, articles of utility or *virtue* in ivory, enamel, silver, copper, iron, terra cotta or paper.[55]

Creswick's signature medium, terra cotta, continued to be commissioned for both large and small projects including delicate portraits, both relief and free-standing. One fine example is 'Miss Mary Creswick, 1897' (recorded as 'presumed' on the Glasgow University Mapping Sculpture Site), a portrait bust in terra cotta now in the Creswick family collection. It is a work of great refinement and beauty, which it captures with a Ruskin-inspired clarity of vision and truth, both in terms of the subject and the medium. Here again we see the 'pure and true genius,' that Ruskin once nurtured, reaching true beauty and full flower.

53 B.M.S.A. (Birmingham Municipal School of Art) Management sub-committee Minutes 10, 1906-1908, Birmingham City University Art and Design Archive, SA/AD/2/10.

54 Ibid.

55 Birmingham Magazine, number 6 vol. 3, 1903. *A Birmingham Sculptor* pp. 173-4.

Creswick also became an associate of the Bromsgrove Guild of Applied Arts, founded by a former pupil of Creswick's and fellow Ruskinian, Walter Gilbert (1871–1946). Creswick participated in practical, commercially successful ventures and collaborative commissions for the Bromsgrove Guild, just as he had for the Century Guild. His connections to the Century Guild and endorsement of Gilbert and the Bromsgrove Guild proved a valuable introduction to architect Edmund Rathbone (active 1891-1911), the Century Guild's representative in Liverpool.[56] The commission for the Unitarian Church in Liscard, near Birkenhead, was one such collaborative work, designed by Waring and Rathbone in 1897. This exquisite gem, although not as colourful as when it was originally designed, is today a beautiful and rich reward for anyone who goes out of their way to visit it, decorated by the Bromsgrove Guild in what should be considered one of their most lovely collaborative projects. Creswick's columns make a significant contribution. The four columns supporting the octagonal tower each carry an allegorical image to represent Meditation, Eloquence, Devotion, and Music. The neck of each of the seven exterior columns carries a different floral design, and the interior of the church features floral capitals to the columns. Also, inside the church, there are two small figures by Creswick on the choir stalls. [57]

A major work which stands out in Creswick's Birmingham years is the terra cotta frieze on the building that housed Dean's House Furnishing and Pitman's Birmingham Vegetarian Hotel and Restaurant in Corporation Street. Dating from 1896, it is an example of his continuing commissions from the architectural and commercial community. This is a sophisticated work, showing architecturally integrated decorative panels which, in his signature style, portray what goes on inside the building. (See the chapter *Key Works*, p. 43.)

Creswick's output continued to include decorative panels and building façades. In his only published lecture (of 1891), he held it was:

> …impossible to overestimate the effect of a systematic application of sculpture to our architecture in making the people familiar with all the events of English History, our achievements by land and sea especially if done by those of our profession of acknowledged ability […] such a system would form a powerful aid to the work of our museums and schools of art. If our students and craftsmen had the advantage of the beautiful language of sculpture expressing constantly the uses of institutions, the labours and achievements of men and cities, then I believe they would soon begin to understand what art meant. The systematic help of sculpture that would appeal to our

---

[56] *By Hammer and Hand*: pp. 72- 3.

[57] A paper on the Church by Mrs Jaqueline Bailey.

understanding would quicken our perceptions and sympathies with all that is noble in our national life, religious, poetic, politic and domestic.[58]

It is clear that Creswick practiced what he preached and his constant flow of commissions show that there was both a public and a commissioning appetite for such works of Art. These include an important sub-genre within Creswick's oeuvre: his war memorials.

The Huddersfield Boer War memorial (1905) was among the first, and we can detect the profound understanding of the grief of War. The figure stands four-square but unbowed, staring out over the veldt with eyes that have seen too much death and destruction. It is an example of Creswick seeing with the 'eyes that Ruskin opened for him,' to paraphrase Charlotte Brontë's words upon reading *Modern Painters* in 1843.[59] Creswick's portrait bust of an officer in the collection of Museums Sheffield, and of George Dawson (my husband's father, who was indeed a tragic figure) to my personal knowledge capture the full impact of their experiences.

The Boldmere memorial is perhaps his most poignant work, simply portraying the lost generation of youth. The tender and insightful sculpture highlights with the utmost delicacy the vulnerability of the boys, and the fragility of the lives that were lost and the generations unborn as a result of the violence of war. No posturing or nationalism is on display, just stark loss. (*Key Works*, page 50)

It was also apparent that the main Birmingham artistic institutions valued Creswick's membership and the vitality it brought to their exhibitions. The Midlands Art Group was the

[58] Creswick, p.217.

[59] W.G Collingwood, *The Life and Work of John Ruskin*, (Methuen, 1893. vol 1) p.162.

first to welcome him as a tutor in 1891, where he taught and gave modelling demonstrations to members until 1926. He was also a professional associate of the Royal Birmingham Society of Artists from 1891 to 1916, and a professional member from 1916 to 1927. He also served as the Society's Professor of Sculpture from 1894 to 1926 and was a member of The Birmingham Art Circle from 1893 to 1908, retaining for some time his associations with The Arts and Crafts Exhibition Society and working on the exhibition committee from 1894 to 1899. His London connections also continued for a few years while he worked to establish himself professionally in the Midlands. His recognition in London was a helpful reminder of his status, and the prestige of having been a London Academy exhibitor would have also enhanced the standing of the Birmingham Art Schools. Creswick exhibited at the Royal Academy Summer Exhibition in 1888 with 'Manly Pride, A Smith at Work;' in 1891 with 'The Young Footballer,' and in 1903 with 'Cheng Keng Luie,' a statue to be cast in bronze for the Engineers' Institute in Penang (right). Finally in 1909, he exhibited 'The Old Potter.' Portraiture, and the life and dignity of the common man, woman and child continued to be the main recurring themes in all his exhibition contributions.

Once more it would appear that Creswick had made the most of his connections, as the commission for the Penang Mandarin could well have resulted from his early days with the Engineering Volunteers in Sheffield, a line of enquiry still in progress.

Creswick's work on public buildings in Birmingham constitutes a substantial part of his output. The Dean and Pitman building is his central work in the city and is discussed in *Key Works* on p. 43. There are, however, several other examples that deserve attention, in particular the decoration of the Library Buildings in Nechells Parkway (1891/3), Handsworth (1891), and Sparkhill (1900). The Bloomsbury Library in Nechells Parkway is a further example of Creswick putting into practice his commitment to depict in art the lives of working folk and children. The six panels are described in *Key Works* on p. 40.

Creswick also produced two narrative panels for Handsworth Library's extension in 1891, an example of his skill as a story-teller, with a tale of steam trains, espionage and mechanical inventions under the title *Scenes from Birmingham's Industrial Past*. Once again we can see the principles he articulated in his lecture expressed in practice, this time to interest, intrigue and inform, almost by stealth, telling the story of James Watt and Mathew Boulton's steam engine in the nearby Soho Foundry, often called the 'cradle of the industrial revolution.'[60] This is perhaps not a subject that would have won Ruskin's approval, given his opposition to the railway, but the skill of the craftsman certainly would have drawn praise. But this pupil was never a slavish follower of the master, something else of which Ruskin would have approved, so a delicate balance was maintained. A description and illustrations follow in *Key Works*, p. 45.

The later Sparkhill panels of 1900 present a far more decorative and restrained depiction, perhaps the result of constraints imposed upon the commission, or possibly the allegorical figures themselves required a different approach to his usual individual depiction. Above the Library window are figures representing *Knowledg*e with the lamp and *Justice* holding a pair of scales and a sword. Over the Building Control office is *History* scribing on a tablet and a further undefined figure depicted wearing a strap or thong (possibly to represent *Retribution*). These figures are apparently non-attributed although Noszlopy commented that 'the style of carving [...] and the sharply rendered and somewhat hectic details, suggest that Creswick was the sculptor.'[61]

The 1920s seem to be Creswick's final working years. He had retired from the School of Art in 1918 and few of his sculptures can be traced to his retirement. The figure of St Michael (1927) seems indicative of a period of understandable reflection after the 1914-1918 war.[62]

With two of his sons in Edinburgh, and the family firm much reduced, Creswick did contemplate another major work for the Worshipful Company of Cutlers in London which had requested preliminary sketches for another frieze on their façade. The project was never carried through, but a maquette dated 1922 survives and shows no diminution of his skills or innovative approach to work. The low relief panel shows the trade in horn which was still a mainstay in the manufacture of cutlery, and scenes of hunting show the extent of its

[60] George Noszlopy, *Public Sculpture of Birmingham Including Sutton Coldfield.* (Liverpool University Press, 1998) p. 118.

[61] Ibid p. 126.

[62] Ogden.

continued use. The panel is fresh and lively with decorative bands of birds and hunting scenes surrounded with almost *art nouveau* foliage. It is a piece that, despite its morally objectionable components of slavery and the killing of animals for vast quantities of horn being traded, still seems to have a certain beauty. Possibly it was the first awakenings of conscience relating to the horn trade that prompted the decision not to commission this work.

Creswick's last and perhaps most surprising work was the 'Stations of the Cross' at the Catholic Church of Our Lady and St Brigid in Northfield, Birmingham. This almost completely unrecorded work has hardly been mentioned apart from in Ogden's exceptionally well-researched paper.[63] He describes it as a masterful finale to his career and suggests they are among his best works. They are a striking and powerful return to his relief works and are considered in *Key Works*, p. 52.

After this final work, Creswick seems to have retired and had a happy life according to *Suttonian*, a correspondent in the local paper. In an article celebrating his 80th birthday, a happy image is presented of a man who, after having had in his early years of work a life expectancy of between thirty and thirty-five years, was enjoying a well-earned retirement. He was a member of The Boldmere Conservative Club, and was described as still riding his bicycle; he played a good game of golf, was an expert angler and could give a few pointers to most men at billiards or snooker. His interest in outdoor sports was evident in his sculptures of sportsmen, and he continued his membership of the Conservative Club until his death.

The tribute by Sir Frank Brangwyn, which will be covered in more detail in the conclusion, speaks of the passing of '…a great figure in Art not only for the work of his hands, but also for the link that he represented with another Master, John Ruskin, and the men who in their association with him did so much to shape the artistic outlook of the late Victorians.'[64] Brangwyn also wrote in a letter of condolence to my grandfather of being 'deeply grieved by the passing of our dear old friend [...] nothing would give me greater pleasure than to honour his memory'[65]

---

[63] Ogden.

[64] *Birmingham Post* February 13, 1946.

[65] Unpublished letter in the family archive held by Peter Murray.

Creswick was ninety three when he died. Ruskin had enabled him to live out a long and fulfilled life, and we are all enriched by the legacy and dedication of a true Ruskinian.

Benjamin Creswick, eightieth birthday portrait, 1943.

Benjamin and his wife Fanny in the garden of their home at Elmwood, Jockey Road, c. 1925.

Key Works

The terra cotta frieze for the Cutlers' Hall, Warwick Lane, London. 1887. (Page 24)

Better the rudest work that tells a story or records a fact, than the richest without meaning. There should not be a single ornament put on great civic buildings, without some intellectual intention.
(*The Seven Lamps of Architecture*, Works 8, 230)

The terra cotta frieze on the façade of the Worshipful Company of Cutlers in Warwick Lane, opened in 1887, is the best known of Benjamin Creswick's works. The frieze is almost 30ft in length, just less than 3ft in height, and includes 33 figures and detailed backgrounds in high relief.

In the tableau we can follow the various stages involved in the manufacturing process. There is a contrast between the rough-hewn representation of the workplace and the delicacy of the figures with a sensitivity of grouping and a narrative flow. This places emphasis on the harshness of working conditions and the vulnerability of the workmen; however physically strong they may be, their work pits them against the raw and elemental nature of the manufacturing process. Water is an ever-present driving force for the machinery, and there is a constant necessity for whetting grindstones and cooling metal blades during forging. Ironically it is also a contributing factor to the lung disease suffered by the workmen. The elements of fire and air are also featured, harnessed to the forge and the smelting processes. The earth is represented by metal ores created in the earth's molten core, the cooling lava and rock strata that formed the grindstones. Creswick's medium of terra cotta represents the very earth itself.

Creswick shows the viewer the energy, vitality and sheer hard work of the workers: tired men, shoulders drooped, beside muscular frames hard at work; old, worn and weary faces beside those of youth, only at the start of their hard life in the heat of the furnace or the noise of the grinding floor. We can learn much about the work process without the need for words.

This is a biographical study from one who once knew this place and its hardships well, and there is no attempt to glamourize the scene. In fact it is thought that the fifth figure from the left in the second detailed panel is a self-portrait of Creswick at the grinding hull.

In December 1888, the *Sheffield and Rotherham Independent* published an article which is descriptive of Creswick and his work, showing the fierce local pride in Benjamin Creswick's origins and his success in the Great Metropolis of London. The words offer an interesting contemporary opinion of the reception of his work:

> Such is the description of our modern frieze, a work which itself is sufficient to make any man famous, and taken in conjunction with the fact that the talent which produced this design is prolific, teeming with subjects of similar vitality and interest, and that the man who possesses this talent has himself sprung from the workmen themselves, it may be we have in our very midst a parallel to Giotto from among his sheep. For Creswick the artist who designed and modelled this frieze, and who also modelled the head of Carlyle on the tablet in Cheyne Walk, is or rather was a Sheffield grinder, a workman working with his hands, and doing in his earlier years similar work to that which he illustrated with such marvellous plastic skill. Imperfections there may be, no doubt; but the true interest and vitality of the work, and the beauty of artistic grouping are not to be gainsaid [...] It is due to the influence of Professor Ruskin's little museum at Sheffield that the genius of the young grinder found its true bent, and received its encouraging direction; and under Professor Ruskin's own guidance, and in diligent study of the great art critic's works, has the young sculptor found his true power.

It is surprising that this spectacular frieze represented Creswick's first major commission, such is the power and maturity of the work. It is rightly considered by many as his masterpiece. Ruskin wrote in his chapter, 'The Nature of Gothic' about bringing forth the majesty of the working man, and this is a prime example of the realisation of Ruskin's words.

The Bloomsbury Library, 1891. (Page 32)

The Bloomsbury Library, Nechells Parkway, Birmingham, is a Grade II Listed Building designed by the architects Cossins and Peacock. Along the main facade of the building are a series of superb buff terra cotta panels that are a further example of Creswick putting into practice his commitment to depict in his art the lives of working folk and children.

The main Panel (above) is an allegorical representation of the city of Birmingham, depicted here as a woman who is both strong and beautiful, reflective of the city Creswick loved and wished to serve. In this one figure, arguably the most 'classical' representation he ever created, he brings these ideals together, while retaining humanity, dignity and inward reflection. The classically draped female holds a crown and a laurel branch, the symbols of victory and achievement in the arts. The figures are surrounded with fruit and flora, as well as armaments, which represent an industry of particular importance to Birmingham.

The smaller panels following represent *Work* of two kinds: *Industrial*, (Creswick's signature image of a forge is central), with two children, a boy and girl studying at each end, and *Rural*, harvesting.

A further two smaller panels (below) represent *Leisure*. In the first panel boys play rugby, cricket and lacrosse. In the second, girls relax outdoors and enjoy the gentler pastime of skipping

The sixth and final panel appears to show three generations of a family enduring sadness with restraint and dignity. Whereas the other panels are straightforward depictions of humanity at work and play, the sadness and realism of this final one requires more thought. Is this the weary and worn labourer near the end of his days, surrounded by his family? The theme seems to emphasise mutual support among and between the generations. Women seem predominant in the caring roles of mother, wife and grandmother with the men seeming to suffer the burdens of needing to support their families by their daily toil.

Noszlopy saw these as contemporary figures; Beattie described them as workaday realism.[66] Creswick himself commented that 'There is never a building in our midst but could be made to sparkle with interest, but could be made of real interest to our children for generations to come.'[67]

As well as the narrative panels discussed, Creswick produced a frieze that runs along the back of the Bloomsbury Library building, made up of ten separate panels.

[66] Beattie S. *The New Sculpture*, New Haven: Yale University, 1983.

[67] National Association for the Advancement of Art and its Application to Industry, Birmingham Meeting of 1891, *(Transactions of).*

The Dean and Pitman Building, 1896. (Page 30, 32)

Dean's House Furnishing and Pitman's Birmingham Vegetarian Hotel and Restaurant in Corporation Street, Birmingham

This commission for double-fronted commercial premises in what was a very prestigious part of Birmingham's city centre was a return to the low relief style of Creswick's successful work on the façade of Heath the Hatters in London. The overall scheme of decoration on this building, however, was much more complex and diverse, involving not only the coat of arms, but the humorous portrayal of the string course with the lifelike treatment of the putti-like figures grasping the ends of this 'string.' Creswick depicted two 'toddlers' which are such realistic portraits that one feels they must have been modelled from his own children. He put his stamp on this low relief buff terra cotta scheme of decoration with his signature portrayal of real workmen and women, and although they may have been somewhat stylised poses, these were still real people, engaged in believable and recognisable work and relaxation leaving no doubt of the truthfulness of the sculptor's intention to engage the passer-by in an understanding of the work on the building.

The free-standing group of figures on the top of the building were added at a slightly later date and represent a rare example of Creswick's ability to exercise his talent in three dimensional life-size works, where once again he shows a complete mastery of his chosen form. The figures are seen celebrating the recent granting of city status to Birmingham, and are real people as well as allegorical figures, rather than the stereotypical figures so often represented on city buildings. Once, more it is truth and vision portrayed through Creswick's individual interpretation of Ruskin's teaching. The two distinctly different businesses that occupied the building are represented on their respective sides: diners at the restaurant in conversation, and furniture-makers in their workshop: Creswick at his very best.

Handsworth Library, 1891. (Page 33)

The first panel depicts a discussion between Watt and Boulton on how to apply rotary motion to the steam engine. However, their conversation was overheard by a servant at the Inn who promptly sold the information to a rival engineer. Only when Watt tried to patent his invention did he discover that he had been cheated of his idea. This is a story with a lesson in 'industrial espionage' that the local children would have enjoyed.

In the decorative band below the panels Creswick has hidden little figures of miners lying in a narrow coal seam with foliage which might, fancifully, represent the vegetative growth that over time had formed the coal seam itself: the motivating power for the steam engine. In this way Creswick gave his audience a geology lesson, too.

A further panel, unfortunately obscured by a lamp above the library entrance and consequently photographed in two sections, depicts the machinery and Watt in conversation with Dr Robinson, showing him a model of the steam train. The work presents a wonderful and engaging pictorial lesson in local history.

Birmingham celebrated the new Handsworth Library building (formerly known as the Council House) in this postcard, c. 1903, which shows the building bright and new, as Creswick would have remembered it.

Wrought Iron Bookstand, 1899.

When J. Thackray Bunce J.P., editor of the *Daily Post* and influential supporter of the Birmingham Municipal School of Art retired in 1899, the school asked Benjamin Creswick to make a wrought iron book stand to present to him. It was a further example of Creswick's continuing desire for innovation. On this occasion his exploration of metalwork, indicative of his enduring interest in the central place of the forge, in both craft and industrial processes: the production of blade and tool, horseshoe and hoe, alongside decorative work. This bookstand, at once enduring and substantial, has the decorative theme of leaves linking it to the leaves of the books it was designed to hold, and is a powerful and complex fusion of form and decoration. It was featured in the *Birmingham Magazine* in 1903 as an example of fine design and craftsmanship.

Repoussé Metalwork

Repoussé copperwork dating to around 1901.

Creswick worked on a number of copper and silver items from the late 1890s. Caskets, jewel cases, cigarette boxes and cigar boxes; all received attention, his innovative eye ensuring some fine decoration.

Several of these items were exhibited, and it appears from information gained from auction records that they were achieving good prices. Both the *Studio* magazine and the *Birmingham Magazine* featured images of his work. They included combinations of copper work with silver fittings, and an unusual copper clock case.

The copper casket (above) has been donated to the Collection of the Guild of St George and it is hoped that an oak lining may be fabricated with wood from the Wyre Forest when the metalwork restoration is complete.

The decorative repoussé work (below) is believed to be part of a decorative scheme by the Bromsgrove Guild for a Liverpool shipping magnate in the early 1900s. A single panel beneath the mantelshelf represents the story of the water spirit Undine. Creswick had earlier provided repoussé ornament as well as cast panels during his collaboration with Mackmurdo, and returned to the skill in later years with an art nouveau feeling in his work.

Bournville, 1905. (Page 26)

Creswick was commissioned to create the decorative stonework on the Bournville Junior School, built between 1902 and 1905. The resident architect for the project, William Alexander Harvey, designed over 500 houses in Bournville between 1895 and 1904, having previously studied at the Birmingham Municipal School of Art. But the crucial Ruskinian link here was almost certainly John Howard Whitehouse, who worked at Cadbury's, and was Secretary of the Ruskin Society of Birmingham and editor of its journal, *Saint George*. He would have been aware of Creswick, and probably knew him and introduced him to Harvey.

The work consists of five decorative panels portraying dancing figures with decorative features that indicate a harvest theme. The fullness of the fruits and vines are combined with a spirited dance, in full expression of the season.

Creswick seems to be in his element as he apparently summons the music and fills the viewer's heart with the joy of the occasion, as these country dancers are swept up in the celebration of a good harvest and the prospect of winter with a full barn and cellar. Carved from Portland stone it is another *tour de force* from a craftsman with full command of his medium.

There are also many decorative details on the walls and around the doors of the school building, including a beautiful little nest full of eggs on the top of an arch over a nearby doorway. All are created with true Ruskinian vigour and although these details do not seem to have been recorded as Creswick's work, they are unmistakably his.

The Boldmere Memorial, 1921. (Page 31)

The clay maquette (above left) was translated to a finished bronze (above right, and below) and unveiled in 1921 as a memorial to those members of the Boldmere Swimming Club who lost their lives in the First World War. In the sensitive interpretation, the figure of an athletic-looking youth is seated on the branch of a tree which forms a rustic base. The young boy is being instructed in the placing of his hands ready for diving into the water. This image speaks of the tender generations lost through war and is evocative of a more innocent time, poignant and stark in its symbolism of loss.

The bronze statue was for many years situated outdoors in Sutton Park and exposed to the weather before being moved inside the entrance of the Wyndley Baths in 1971 where it has since endured the chlorine fumes, accounting for its degraded patina.

Paper Frieze c.1900.

The Birmingham-based architectural partnership of Crouch and Butler worked in an arts and craft style that favoured the Old English revival. They often featured friezes high on the walls of their rooms using plaster modelled in high relief, or coloured stencil designs on woven fabrics. Tighter budgets called for such friezes to be printed on wallpaper using wood blocking for the decoration. This suited Creswick's style perfectly and he frequently worked for them, and later also for the Manchester-based company, Goodall & Son for whom he carried out similar work. His lifelong friend Frank Brangwyn records that Creswick designed and constructed a machine that could print the wood-blocked images on a continuous roll of paper up to 170 feet in length without repetition of the images.

An example of these friezes has survived and was part of the Creswick family collection. It was presented in 2000 by Mrs Joy Murray to the Collection of the Guild of St George

Information from the conservators indicates that the surviving sections were made in the factory of Goodall & Son in Manchester during the last decade of the 19th century. They felt the condition suggested that the friezes had never been attached to a wall or been exhibited.

Interestingly, one section has a manufacturer's stamp which contains the information 'Ben Creswick & Sons, 22 (it should have read 26) Great Charles Street, Birmingham' where the family lived between 1897 and 1903.

Detail from frieze printed for Goodall & Son, Manchester.

'Stations of the Cross.' Catholic Church of Our Lady and St Brigid, Northfield, Birmingham, 1929. (Page 34)

Creswick's last and perhaps most dramatic project stands apart from his other undertakings as it is the only major religious work he produced. The fourteen panels at the Catholic Church of Our Lady and St Brigid, Northfield, Birmingham are powerful, evocative sculptures in deep relief buff terra cotta. The backgrounds are suggestive of renaissance period landscapes but the figures are detailed and compelling, every bit as humanly real as the figures he produced for the Cutlers Frieze in London forty years earlier.

Each panel is signed and dated, with dates ranging from 1920 to 1929, although by far the majority have the latter date. Simon Ogden suggests that the work was not originally intended for this church, and the gaps in the dating suggest that an earlier project was abandoned, but then taken up by the Northfield Church in 1929, although so far it has not been possible to access relevant records. But whatever their history, it is difficult to stand before such beautiful and dramatic depictions without feeling the interpretive power of the sculptor's craft.

Conclusion

If we are to draw a conclusion about Benjamin Creswick's place in Ruskin's rich legacy, we must first acknowledge Ruskin's estimate of the 'true genius' he discerned in Creswick's early work, and the desire he had to see Creswick develop as an artist. With a wider knowledge of Ruskin's thoughts, expressed through his correspondence, a fuller picture emerges. Letters held in the archives of the Rosenbach Library in Philadelphia and the Ruskin Library at Lancaster, together with the recent work by Mark Frost on the curators of the Walkley Museum, Henry and Emily Swan, considerably enrich our knowledge.

It has been observed that of Creswick's many lectures, just one has survived in written form. This suggests that he was more of a practical 'hands-on' man than a writer, but that one record does give a wonderful insight to his thoughts, suggesting that many of his lectures were spontaneous and engaging expressions of his teaching,

From these sources we are able to gain a privileged view of the development of Creswick's skills. It was Creswick's background as a worker in the grinding hulls of Sheffield's cutlery trade and his declining health that spurred his desire for release. It was his ready access to the Walkley-based Museum that drew him onward, as one of the working men for whom it was built, with its granary of inspiring and edifying treasure.

Ogden saw Creswick as a paragon of Ruskin's values. In my subsequent research, I have come more and more to see this as a major facet of Creswick's work. But with equal interest, I also see Creswick acknowledged as a successful example of Ruskin's relationship with the working men with whom he came into contact, and of whom he often wrote, whether individual artists or men he met through his teaching at the London Working Men's College. But in contrast to many of those young men, Creswick remained to some extent 'his own man' – not only in the sense that he worked as a sculptor, metal worker, stone carver, bronze founder *and* designer – but in that he later found a lifetime of work entirely independent of Ruskin's earlier patronage.

Ruskin's vision for Creswick had been for an apprenticeship in a single discipline, although he encouraged both Creswick's terra cotta work and his stone-carving skills. We know from Ruskin's own writing that having observed his 'true and pure genius' he invested time and energy 'setting Creswick on his path in work and thought.' Edith Hope Scott described Creswick's early endeavours at Bewdley and Beaucastle as work which was delightful both to the sculptor and everyone who saw it – perhaps a Ruskinian enjoinder to create and perceive art with, and for joy.

Creswick had experience of life within an artisan family, to which he added the tough personal experience of the knife grinder's work. We might expect his output to be biased towards the hard, heavy, industrial scenes, but with Ruskin's influence and inspired love of nature, we see in Creswick's work a clear understanding of beauty as well as harshness. The evidence in Ruskin's letter to Creswick of 1878 (p.17) where he writes of 'having more to say to Creswick than any other of his friends and to rejoice in Creswick's success' indicates the strong bond of understanding and affection Ruskin felt for his protégé, and the influence of Ruskin's teaching on Creswick.

Although Creswick remained in his element as a sculptor working in terra cotta till the end of his career, he continually explored the possibilities of other materials. Stone should be acknowledged as his second favourite medium, a thorough understanding of which had been recognised by Ruskin with his early determination to set Creswick carving on his visionary museum building (p.19). That Creswick also cast his work in bronze, unusual for a sculptor, is tribute to his versatility and the constant quest for new knowledge and a determination to refine his teaching abilities. He also experimented with the use of copper, silver, brass and combinations of various metals.

This was also recognised and fostered by Ruskin at an early stage, as illustrated in his letter to Emily Swan in 1877. He had said that Creswick was in no danger of being 'conceited' by having marble bought for him 'because he is always striving to do more than he is able for, and will be kept modest by increasing success.'[68]

Creswick's work continued to develop from that first large commission in London for the Worshipful Company of Cutlers, with its elemental truth and moving portraits of his Sheffield colleagues. There can be little doubt that his body of work would have gone on to be even greater had he not chosen also to teach, but having experienced the practical difficulties of craftsmen in their struggle to get an honest return for their work, and having benefitted from Ruskin's patronage, he chose to pass his skills and experience on to future generations.

Although there has not as yet been a full artistic and historical evaluation of Creswick's work, a comprehensive illustrated catalogue in

[68] Rosenbach *Unpublished Letters from John Ruskin to Henry and Emily Swan 1877-1878, Volume VI* [EL3. R956 MS1, v.6] 1877.

preparation, showing both the works currently recorded and others continually being discovered, will honour a true master craftsman.

A tribute written for the Birmingham Post dated February 13th 1946 by Sir Frank Brangwyn R.A. celebrating Creswick's life is a touching testament to a long-lasting friendship. He writes of John Ruskin remaining a poignant influence throughout the sculptor's life, and of Creswick's work with Selwyn Image and others who also kept alive the teaching and ideals of Ruskin. He remembers as a boy visiting Creswick's Studio at Newman Street in London and seeing the great figure of 'Humanity' undertaken for the Positivist Church. Some years later, in 1864, he lodged in Creswick's Newman Street flat.[69] That Brangwyn was familiar with Creswick's London and Birmingham works seems to indicate his keen interest in following his friend's career, even when he 'went to live in the provinces,' a telling turn of phrase signifying the yawning gulf he perceived between London and the Midlands that persists even today in some circles, but was even more widespread then. However, Brangwyn managed to bridge the invisible divide and they remained friends. His tribute was comprehensive, containing references to Creswick's teaching career and pointing out that many of his pupils had become successful sculptors, and that it was ostensibly due to his keen interest that the School of Art was enlarged. Creswick, he commented, was also a potter, a metal worker and a printer 'designing and making the blocks and the machine to print a frieze on agricultural subjects, 170-feet long without repeat – a feat hitherto unknown in the printing world'. He also mentions that Creswick was survived by four sons and two daughters, five of whom were carrying the torch of art and craft, although with the exception of Charles and John any information is sparse.

Creswick was also the subject of a family tribute from Edith Clews, one of Fanny and Ben's children, a tribute which was preserved by his son, my grandfather, which describes him as a '<u>most</u> wonderful father, a great sculptor, [with] an unending ability to design.'

My own research has been undertaken in tribute to Benjamin Creswick, and increasingly over the years, John Ruskin. I felt a special and personal pleasure at the 2015 launch of *Ruskin in Sheffield* where I spent a rewarding evening among the feast of interesting projects, both seeing and sharing the enthusiasm engendered by the displayed image of my great grandfather's Cutlers Hall frieze. The Community Hall in Walkley was full of enthusiastic, interested people engaging with both

---

[69] http:// www.frankbrabngwyn.org

the sculpture and its history. Creswick and Ruskin were clearly still capturing the imaginations of the people of Sheffield. Their comments and questions, and their growing appreciation of their city's heritage, reminded me of my grandfather's conversation with the never-ending stream of people who visited his studio. I could imagine the three of them that evening, standing quietly in Walkley, delighted to know that their life and work still opens minds and introduces people to a love of the arts, and in particular, the appreciation of sculpture.

Timeline

1853
Benjamin Creswick born.

1860
Benjamin Creswick apprenticed as a knife grinder.

1873
Benjamin Creswick married Fanny Goodhall.

1874
First child (William) born in Sheffield.

1876
Second child (Edward) born Sheffield.
First exhibition with the Sheffield Society of Artists.

1877
Swan visited Brantwood to present Creswick's case to Ruskin.
Creswick visited Brantwood working on the Ruskin Bust.
Ruskin began financial support of Creswick.

1878
Third child (Benjamin) born at Bewdley.

1879
Bust of Ruskin presented to Prince Leopold at the Walkley Museum.
Benjamin Creswick attended the inaugural meeting of the Guild of St George in Birmingham.
Creswick among young artists entertained by Ruskin at Brantwood.
The Creswick family lodged at Coniston.

1880
Creswick lived in the Mackmurdo household at Fitzroy Street, London.

1881
Fourth child (John) born in Sheffield.

1882
Worked in Sheffield and London.
Portrait Bust of Mackmurdo.
Creswick became a member the Sheffield Ruskin Society.

1883
Fifth child (Charles) born in Enfield, Middlesex.

1884
Exhibited at Walker Art Gallery, Liverpool, and at the Enfield Exhibition.

1885
Sixth child (Mary Ellen) born in Enfield.
Produced model of Carlyle portrait roundel.

1886
Became Associate of the Century Guild.
Exhibited at Walker Art Gallery, Liverpool.
Frank Brangwyn visited Creswick in his Newman Street studio.
Creswick provided the decorative metal work for the Mackmurdo Buffet which would be exhibited in Manchester 1887/8.

1887
Worshipful Company of Cutlers Frieze, London, 1887-1888.
Frieze for Heath the Hatters, Oxford Street, London 1887-1888.
Exhibited with the Century Guild at the Royal Jubilee Exhibition, Manchester where Creswick gave modelling demonstrations.
Employed by Goodall, the Century Guild's Agent in Manchester.

1888
Seventh child (Edith) born in Manchester.
Exhibited with the Arts and Crafts Exhibition Society.
Exhibited in the Summer Exhibition Royal Academy of Arts London.
Exhibited at the Walker art Gallery Liverpool.

1889
Exhibited at Leeds City Art Gallery.
Exhibited twice with the Arts and Crafts Exhibition Society.
Appointed Head teacher of modelling and modelling design at the Birmingham Municipal School of Art.

1890
Eighth child (Godfrey) born in Sutton Coldfield, Birmingham.
Exhibited at Leeds City Art Gallery.
Bloomsbury Library terra cotta panels 1891-3.
Commenced modelling demonstrations.

1891
Tutor at Midlands Art Club 1891 until 1926.
Elected professional associate member of the Royal Birmingham Society of Artists 1891-1916.
Exhibited at the Summer Exhibition, Royal Academy of Arts, London.

1892
Exhibited with the Royal Birmingham Society and would continually annually until 1927.

1893
Worked on *Allegories of the Arts*, for the Margaret Street extension to the Birmingham Municipal School of Art.
Member of the Birmingham Art Circle 1893-1908.

1894
Member of the Arts and Crafts Exhibition Society.
Professor of Sculpture at the Royal Birmingham Society of Artists until 1926.

1895
Exhibited at the Walker Gallery. Liverpool.

1896
Frieze and allegorical statues for Dean's House Furnishing and Pitman's Birmingham Vegetarian Hotel and Restaurant in Corporation Street, Birmingham.
Exhibited at the Birmingham Art Circle.

1897
Portrait bust of Miss Mary Creswick.

1899
The Wallasey Memorial Unitarian Church; collaboration on the overall design and worked with the Bromsgrove Guild on exterior stonework and carved wooden pew ends.
Exhibited at the Birmingham Art Circle.

1900
Decorative panels for the Sparkhill Library, Birmingham.
Exhibited at the Birmingham Art Circle.

1901
Worked with metal on decorative items.
Exhibited at the Birmingham Art Circle.

1903
Exhibited at Leeds City Art Gallery.
Exhibited Summer Exhibition, Royal Academy of Arts, London.
Life size study of Cheng Keng Luie executed in bronze for the Engineers Institute, Penang, Malaya.

1905
South African war memorial, Huddersfield.

1909
Exhibited at Summer Exhibition, Royal Academy, London.

1914
Two sons, Charles and John went to Edinburgh to work.

1916
Elected a professional member of Royal Birmingham Society of Artists, and would continue until 1927.

1918
Retired from the Birmingham Municipal School of Art.

1920
The Boldmere War Memorial for the Boldmere Swimming Club, Sutton Coldfield, Birmngham.

1922
Bournville stone sculpture of Dancers.
Commenced work on the *Stations of the Cross* for the Catholic Church of Our Lady and St Brigid, Northfield, Birmingham.
Produced maquette for Worshipful Company of Cutlers proposed second frieze.

1926
Retired from the Midlands Arts Club, and as Professor of Sculpture at the Royal Birmingham Society of Artists.

1927
Creswick retired from the Royal Birmingham Society of Artists.

1929
Completed the panels for the Stations of the Cross.

1931
Fanny Creswick died.

1946
Benjamin died at Jockey Road, Sutton Coldfield, Birmingham.

Publications from the Guild of St George

The Ruskin Lecture: Original Series

1978 Lord Asa Briggs
1979 Robert Hewison: Art & Society. Ruskin in Sheffield in 1876
1981 Philip Rawson: Ruskin, Turner and Time
1982 Van Akin Burd: Ruskin, Lady Mount Temple and the Spiritualists
1982 Michael Kitson: Ruskin's 'Stones of Venice'
1983 Joe Holyoak: J. H. Chamberlain. Ruskin's architect of the Civic Gospel
1985 Anthony Harris: Why do our little girls have large shoes?
1986 Tim Hilton: Ruskin's Masterpiece
1987 Sir Roy Shaw: The Relevance of Ruskin
1988 Nicholas Shrimpton: Ruskin and 'War' [published 2014]
1991 Anthony Harris: Ruskin and Siena
1992 Malcolm Cole: Be like Daisies
1994 Royal W. Leith III: Ruskin and his American followers in Tuscany

The Ruskin Lecture: New Series

2005 Stephen Wildman: Thomas Matthews Rooke [published 2013]
2006 Sam Smiles: Ruskin and Cambridge
2007 Jacqueline Yallop: Our Power to Bequeath
2008 Paul Tucker: Charles Fairfax Murray and Duccio's *Maesta*
2009 Robert Hewison: Of Ruskin's Gardens
2010 Stuart Eagles: Ruskin and Tolstoy
2011 Zoe Bennett: The True Use of Faith
2012 Howard Hull: Demeter's Dowry: Ruskin and Landscape
2013 Mark Frost: Curator and Curatress: The Swans and St George's Museum
2014 Gray Brechin: 'Necessitous Men Are Not Free Men': Bridging Ruskin's Thought and the New Deal

Whitelands Ruskin Lecture

2014 Dinah Birch: Thinking Through the Past: John Ruskin and the Whitelands College May Festival
2015 Sara Atwood: 'An enormous difference between knowledge and education': What Ruskin Can Teach Us

Occasional Lectures and Other Publications

2007 Peter Wardle and Cedric Quayle: Ruskin and Bewdley

2010 James S. Dearden: John Ruskin's Guild of St George

2013 James S. Dearden (ed.): The Roll of Companions of the Guild of St George

2014 Clive Wilmer: 'A new road on which the world should travel': John Ruskin, 'The Nature of Gothic' and William Morris (William Morris Birthday Lecture)

2015 Sara Atwood: 'The earth-veil': Ruskin and Environment (A lecture given at Brantwood)

2015 Stuart Eagles: Miss Margaret E. Knight and St George's Field, Sheepscombe

2015 Annie Creswick Dawson with Paul Dawson: Benjamin Creswick

The Guild also publishes a wide selection of greetings and Christmas cards based on artworks in the Ruskin Collection.

www.guildofstgeorge.org.uk/shop

The Guild of St George was formally established by John Ruskin in 1878. Through the Guild, Ruskin strove to make Britain a pleasanter and happier place in which to live. His aims and aspirations for the Guild are contained in the ninety six "Letters" of his *Fors Clavigera*.

Today the Guild is a charitable Education Trust which tries to put Ruskin's ideas into practice. It owns and supports the Ruskin Collection, housed in Sheffield's Millennium Gallery, and is currently running a series of activities and events in a community heritage project, *Ruskin-in-Sheffield*, supported by the Heritage Lottery Fund. It can offer scholarships and awards across a range of subjects close to Ruskin's heart, including the practice of crafts and scholarly work in agricultural science and economics, education, industry and the social sciences.

The first of the Ruskin Triennial Exhibitions, which focused on the Environment and Sustainability, was shown at Sheffield between October 2009 and January 2010. A second exhibition, with the theme Landscape and Creativity, took place in 2013 and a third is planned on the theme of Craft, to open in the Millennium Galleries Sheffield in 2016.

The Guild is also supporting work on the sustainable development of the Wyre Forest, where it owns farmland, orchards, and 100 acres of woodland. It is regenerating old orchards and hay meadows, renovating and improving its properties, and exploring new projects and programmes of activity.

www.guildofstgeorge.org.uk